THE Journal: DEAR FUTURE II

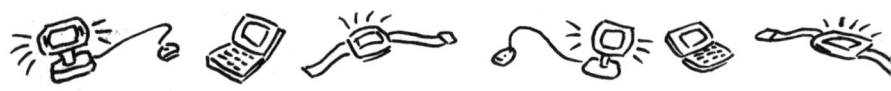

> *Earth time : 1600 hours*
> *Wednesday : May 10, 2198*
>
> **Instructions to Personal Data Assistant**
>
> *Record thought waves as transmitted, translate to text, and post to learning-center bulletin board for transmission to learning centers in other districts.*

Hi. I'm Anika from Unit #2779369K, Chinchilla District. I am transmitting this bulletin in case there are other kids *Out There* who are interested in the study of the past, as I am.

My learning center has just discovered something so wonderful, so solar, that I wanted to share it with other people. I'm still finding it hard to believe myself!

This year, Viki, the group leader at our learning center, decided that our class should make a special study of past civilizations. She ordered some SIMs, or simulated images that are like virtual reality, from the bank at the capital. Then we were able to find out what it was like to live in different stages of Earth's history. Solar!! SIMs are great.

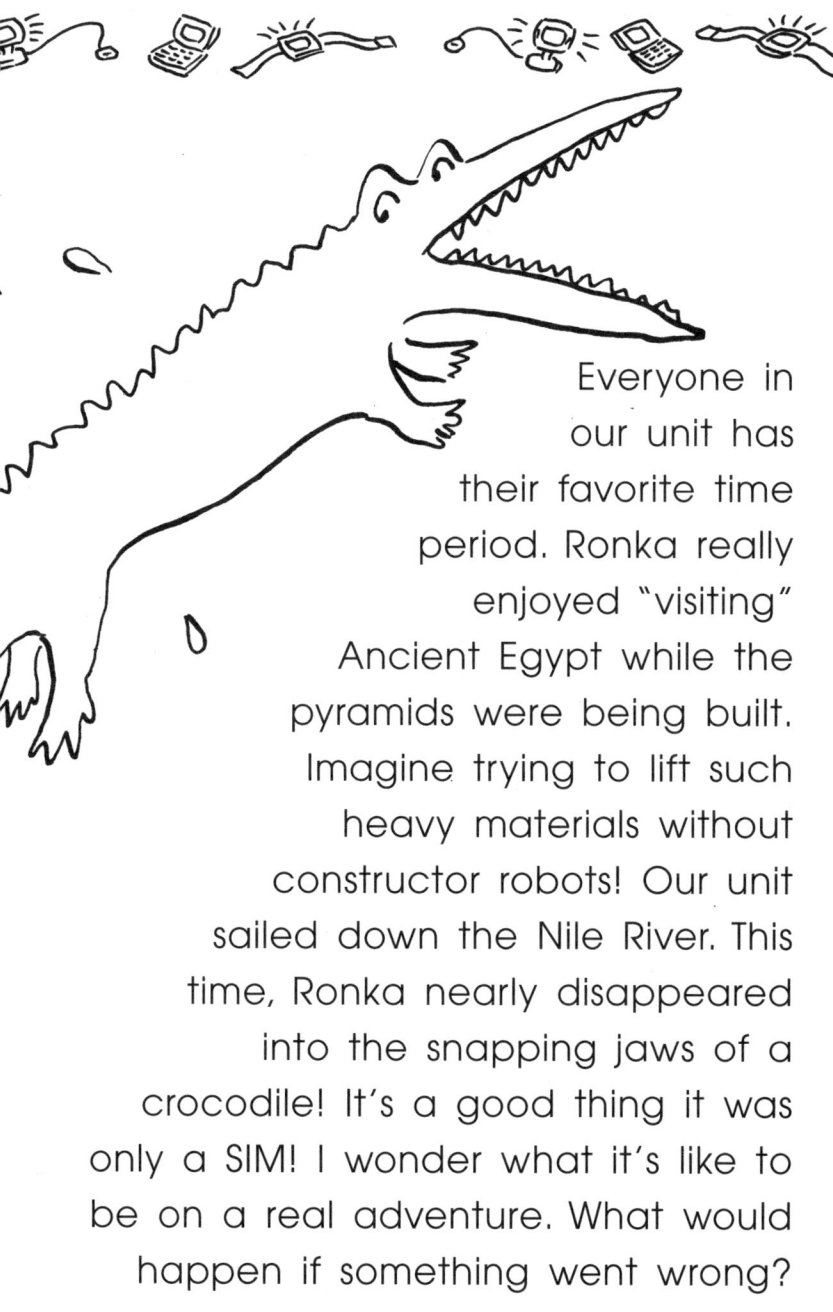

Everyone in our unit has their favorite time period. Ronka really enjoyed "visiting" Ancient Egypt while the pyramids were being built. Imagine trying to lift such heavy materials without constructor robots! Our unit sailed down the Nile River. This time, Ronka nearly disappeared into the snapping jaws of a crocodile! It's a good thing it was only a SIM! I wonder what it's like to be on a real adventure. What would happen if something went wrong?

I decided I wanted to try a different project. Of course, I like visiting different stages of Earth's history, but I don't really feel like I know any of the people. And that doesn't make those places feel very real to me.

So, instead, I scrolled through a data bank and found a feature on family trees. And guess what I found out – people once lived together in families, not in a unit with other children, as we do now. In this feature you could find out who you were related to, going back for years, even centuries! They had names like grandmother or great-aunt. And many people in the families seemed to share a common last name called a surname. None of them had unit numbers, or any number at all.

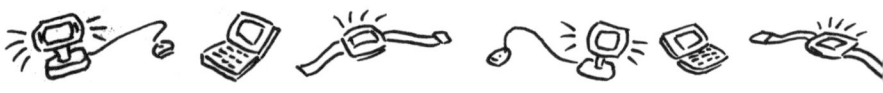

Then I started thinking, wouldn't it be great if I could trace my family tree? I could find out about people who might be a little bit like me. You see, the feature explained that people in families had similarities, because they had similar genes. Now, if I could trace my family tree, I might find someone who liked the things I do.

Anyway, I better explain why I'm posting this bulletin. Yesterday, Viki told us the most galactic thing. Some constructor robots were drilling near the foundations of the learning unit when they found a strange object. Like all constructor robots, they have been programed to report any objects that are not in their data banks. That's why they brought the object to central control for analysis.

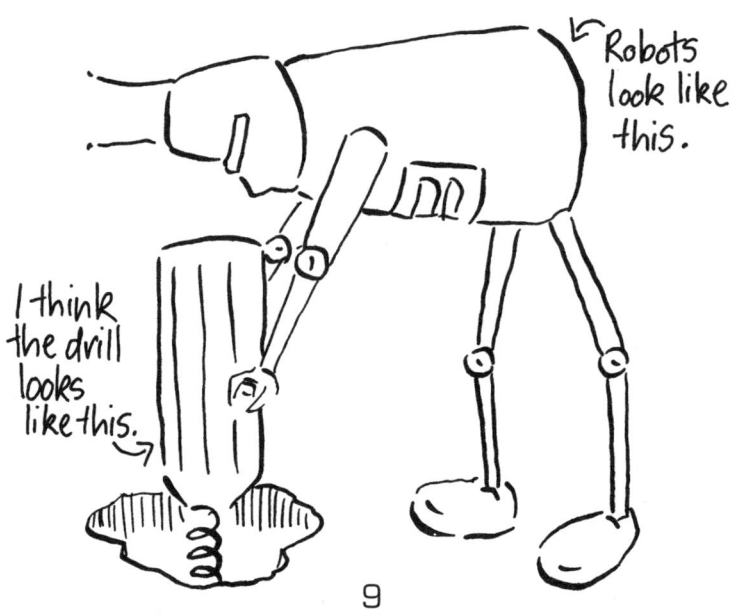

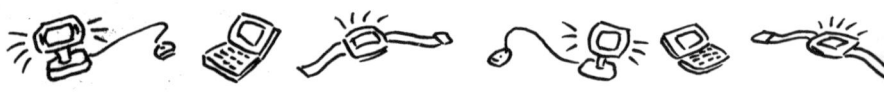

Well, the controller employed a drone robot to use its X-ray vision to scan the contents of the object, just in case it contained anything dangerous. It received a safe readout, so it was authorized to open the object (which Viki said was called a box).

When the controller discovered what was inside the box, she contacted Viki. And this morning, our class looked inside the box! Oh, it was full of amazing things that I've never seen before – except on ROM (read-only memory) discs, of course. There were books! Books haven't been around for about a hundred years. And there were large pieces of flimsy material called paper, with two-dimensional pictures marked on them, and smaller pieces of paper, with faded markings.

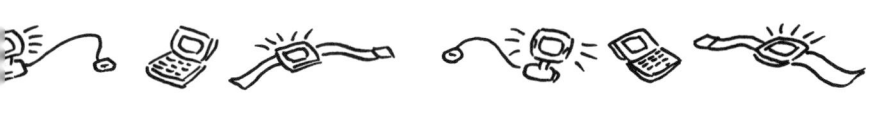

Viki arranged for the small papers to be sent to the restoration lab so we can scan them for ourselves. Imagine being able to hold text in your hands rather than hearing it through speakers or viewing it on a screen!

There were also some two-dimensional pictures of people wearing strange body coverings, and some very antiquated objects containing a substance called tape. Viki said these were called videos. She has sent them to a media expert, who will translate them so we can view them on one of our multiscreens. I wonder what images they contain. Jupiter's moons – I can't wait until tomorrow to find out!

Anika : End of bulletin : 1621 hours

> *Earth time : 1600 hours*
> *Thursday : May 11, 2198*
>
> ### Instructions to Personal Data Assistant
> *Record thought waves as transmitted, translate to text, and post to learning-center bulletin board for transmission to learning centers in other districts.*

Hi. It's Anika again, from Unit #2779369K, continuing my bulletin from yesterday. I've checked my response bank. Thanks to all of you who sent me messages, especially Sweda and Roq.

14

It's good to know that there are others who are interested in the past. We're not encouraged to talk about *Old World*, because the life we have now is the best it has ever been in Earth's history. No one is homeless or hungry or without work, like some of the people we saw in a SIM about the twentieth century. Despite that, I still wonder about my ancestors.

This morning, Viki had the translated and reprogramed material for us to view. And, Jupiter's moons, it's solar!

The box is called a time capsule. We thought it must have come from a very advanced civilization. Even our scientists haven't figured out how to entrap time in a capsule – yet! But there was a handwritten message on the front of it that read:

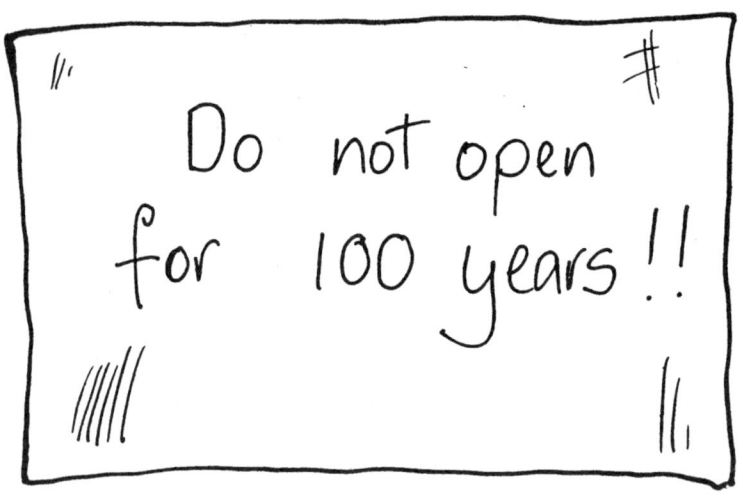

And inside there was material from the year 1998. Two hundred years ago! It sat there for a hundred

years longer than anyone had planned – right through the Great Wars of the 2130s, the Centaurian Invasions of the 2160s, and the Rebuild of 2173. It's a good thing the constructor robots found it!

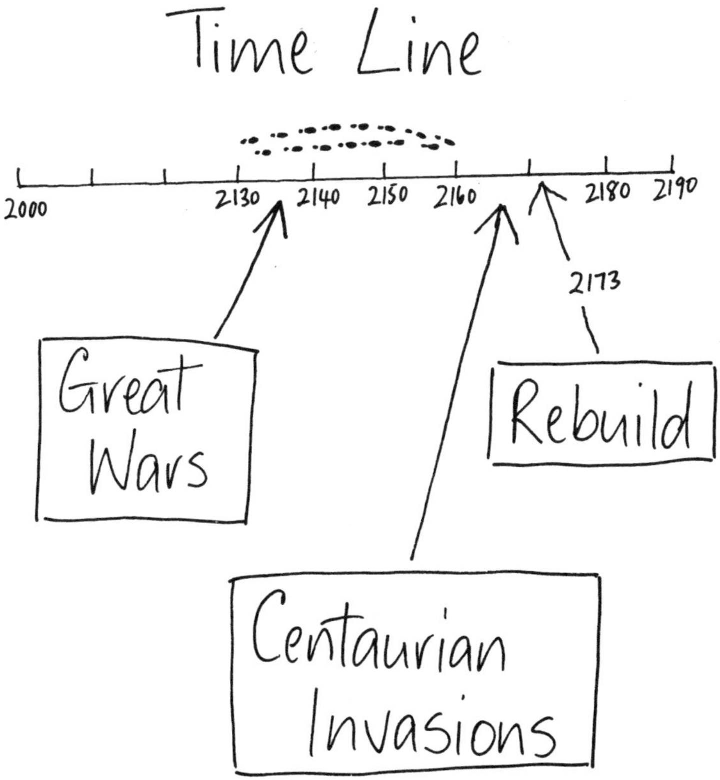

Time Line

The box was buried by some children from a place called a school, as part of a "class" project. The name of their school was Chinchilla! And my unit is in the Chinchilla District. There was a song on one of the videos called the *Chinchilla School Rap* – such strange music! The kids kept saying the school was cool. Perhaps they didn't have climate control like we do now, poor things. Maybe that's why they had to wear so many body coverings.

Inside the time capsule were all sorts of strange things. But the strangest of all was the thing called a journal. Viki told us it was like a day-to-day record of all the things that happened in people's lives and their thoughts and comments about all kinds of things.

It was written by a girl about my age, named Anna. *Anna Loredana Eugenia Hope Reynard.* Such a long name! She even lived in a family with her mother, father, brother, and grandmother. Only five people in one living center! Just imagine how much space they must have had!

I would love to have a brother. Or even a sister. But I know that won't happen now that we keep our population stable. I'd love to be able to talk to someone else who is a bit like me. Wouldn't you?

← Anna's journal

Reading Anna's journal gave me a wonderful idea. I'm going to start one of my own. I will just thought-transfer it to my PDA during personal-interest hour. I'd much rather do that than run around with the others, playing a game of hover hockey or visiting the virtual-reality-games mall. It's such a galactic idea – I just hope I can put it all together.

Well, I have to sign off now and return to the learning center. So happy dreams, my new friends!

Anika : End of bulletin : 1614 hours

Earth time : 1702 hours
Thursday : May 11, 2198

Instructions to Personal Data Assistant

Record thought waves as transmitted, translate to text in all Earth languages, and store on long-lasting FIP discs for retrieval in the year 2298

Dear Future,

This is my very first journal, so I hope I'll record the correct sort of data. Then again, I hope you'll be able to retrieve it! My PDA will translate the data into all current Earth languages.

Here at my learning center we speak two languages, English and Mondo – the global language that people on each continent learn. Do you still speak Mondo?

Before I go any further, I'd better explain to you about my PDA. The letters stand for Personal Data Assistant, and it's like a portable communication tool. When I want to record something, I activate my PDA, which is attached to my wrist. It picks up my thought waves, translates them into text, and then beams them to a communication outlet, such as the learning-center bulletin board. Then, anyone can scan my thought waves.

my PDA

I've arranged for my PDA to store this journal on an indelible FIP disc. I have galactic plans for this disc. I'm going to put it in a time capsule! And I hope someone will find it in one hundred years.

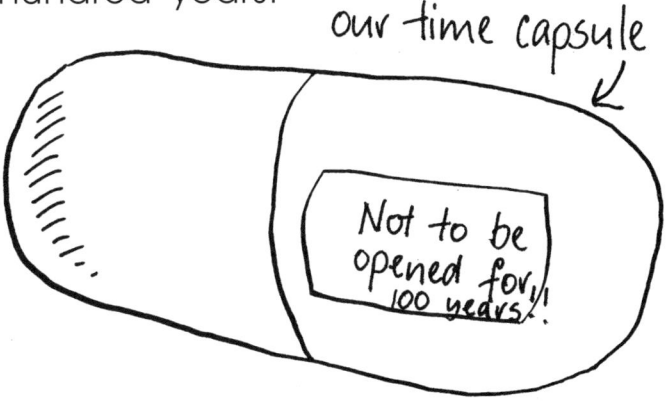

I'm doing this because we found a time capsule under our learning unit. It belonged to some children from two hundred years ago. They filled it with data about what their life was like.

Viki, our group leader, translated the data so that it could be read by our equipment. I'm going to arrange for a disc with some of this data to be included in my time capsule, so you can see some of the things from Anna's time, like really old images called photographs. I'll tell you about what life is like here, in my time. I'm sure you'll think our life now is very strange, just as my learning center did when we read Anna's journal.

For a start, Anna's life and my life are totally different. Anna talked about living with her family, and having parents who went out to work. We don't do that here at the unit. Of course, we all have parents, but we don't see them every day like Anna used to.

my mom and dad

We send our parents bulletins all the time, and they visit us a couple of times a year. Then, we have parents' day. I love parents' day. We all wait in the visitors' room in the learning center until our parents arrive, and then we spend the whole day with them.

Last year, my mother was in China. She was organizing a team to construct a dam. And my father was in Egypt. He was helping to collect records of ancient civilizations so that they could be translated into electronic data and stored on FIP discs in central archives. Dad showed me a piece of stone that was covered with some very strange markings called hieroglyphs.

I want to do something really special for the next parents' day. So I've decided to try and write them a rap, sort of like the one that Suzie and Sharon, from Anna's school, wrote for their school concert.

Today, I went to the music archives and found a sound bite of music from the 1990s, so I could hear what rap music sounded like. Very strange! Anyway, I decided to write a rap about a space race, which is a very popular sport here at the moment.

my mom in China ↓

my dad ↑ in Egypt

Chinchilla Space Rap

Listen up, people
Got a song about space
Going to tell you the story
Of a great space race

Space race – Chinchilla
Space race – Chinchilla

The ships line up
One day at nine
You can hear them roar
Right down the line

Space race – Chinchilla
Space race – Chinchilla

First stop Venus
Next stop Mars
Then off to tag
The moon and stars

Space race – Chinchilla
Space race – Chinchilla

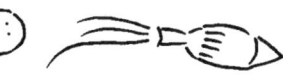 

Starship Alpha
Is in the lead
Its engines firing
At full speed

Space race – Chinchilla
Space race – Chinchilla

Starship Beta
Is also fast
It catches Alpha
And zooms on past

Space race – Chinchilla
Space race – Chinchilla

But Starship Ace
Takes our first place
It's the fastest coolest
Ship in space!

Space race – Chinchilla
Space race – Chinchilla

You know, when I read the words to the rap in Anna's time capsule, I realized she seemed to be having much more fun than we do. They actually had real animals in their class, not just holograms!

I've instructed my PDA to prepare a feature for you. I've supplied it in a number of different formats, including two-dimensional form, because I'm not sure what retrieval systems you'll be using in a hundred years.

Anyway, I have to stop recording now. It's time for colony studies. I'll record more in my personal-interest hour tomorrow.

Anika : End of message

UNIT LIFE

Birth to two years

Children live in Nursery Sector.
Nursery robots train them to walk and talk.

Two to five years

Children move to Kindergarten Sector.
Play robots organize activities.

UNIT LIFE

Five to ten years

Children move to Junior Training Units.
Children learn to operate equipment and use SIMs to study the world outside.

Eleven to fifteen years

Teenagers move to Senior Training Units.
Teenagers train to take on future roles in society.

> *Earth time : 1600 hours*
> *Friday : May 12, 2198*
>
> ***Instructions to Personal Data Assistant***
> *Record thought waves as transmitted, translate to text, and post to learning-center bulletin board for transmission to learning centers in other districts.*

Hi. It's Anika here again. Hi to all my new friends, Sweda, Roq, Jamal, and Nyoc. I love checking my response bank and finding it jammed full of new messages!

No one in my learning center wants to help, so why don't some of you send me some data to put in my time capsule? Let's replicate some of Anna's classmates' ideas. One boy put together a transportation project. They had such Plutonian ideas! Everything in his project used fossil fuels. Imagine using gasoline rather than solar energy. It must be decades since Earth's fossil fuels ran out.

a very old plane →

A girl from Anna's class did a project on her favorite foods. Can you believe people actually used to construct their own food? I once tried to peek into the food lab, but a robot guard shooed me away. It must have been worried I'd contaminate the capsules!

There were lots of other different projects, too. Data about the type of body coverings they wore (scratchy!), and the games they used to play. It looks like they were allowed to play games whenever they wanted to – not just in their personal-interest time.

Another girl wrote about the different collections she had. There were shells, coins, stamps, and magnets. We can't really keep personal possessions in our units, because we don't have enough space in our cubicles. Is it the same for other people?

So if anyone out there would like to contribute data to my time capsule, please advise your PDA to contact mine at Cubicle 47, Sector 813, Unit #2779369K. Good-bye to all my friends *Out There!*

Anika : End of bulletin : 1616 hours

41

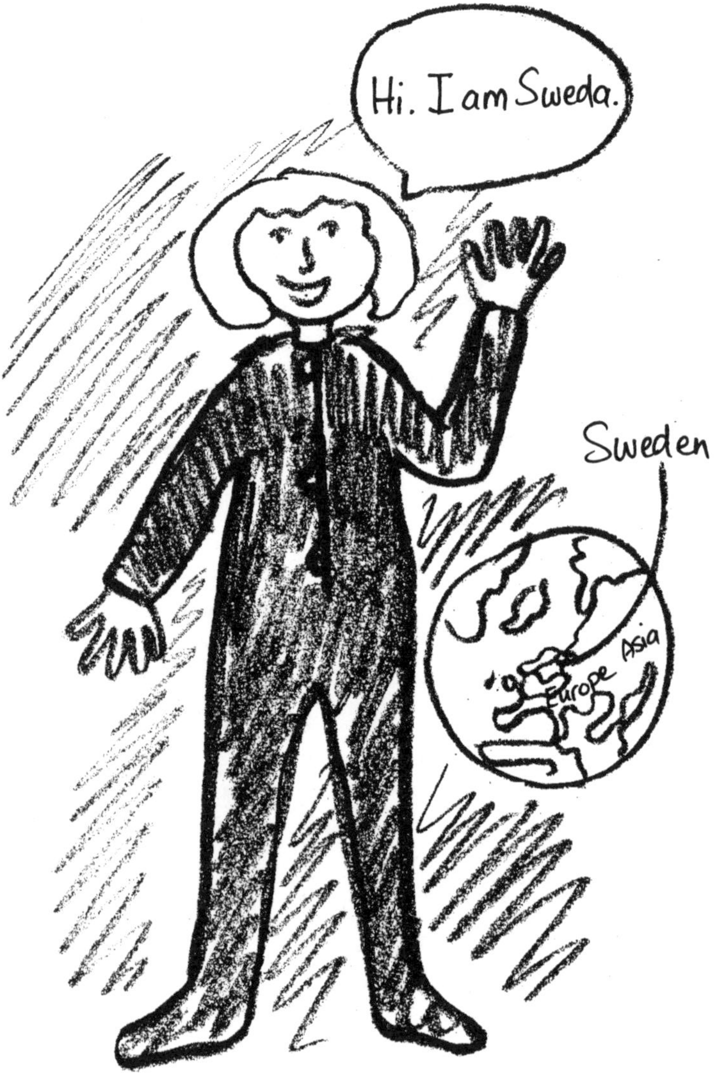
Hi. I am Sweda.
Sweden
Asia
Europe

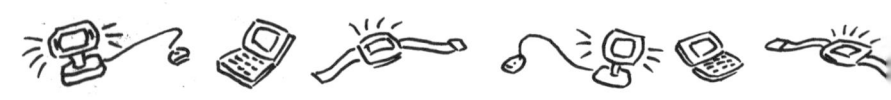

> *Earth time : 0900 hours*
> *Saturday : May 13, 2198*
> *To Anika : Cubicle 47 :*
>   *Sector 813 : Unit #2779369K*
> *From Sweda : Cubicle 14 :*
>   *Sector 923 : Unit #7399982D*
>
> ***Instructions to Personal Data Assistant***
> *Translate from Swedish to English and alert user to existence of incoming message.*

Hi, Anika. Sweda here! Thanks for all the great bulletins you've been sending out. I was so excited when I realized there was someone else *Out There* who liked finding out about the past.

I've read all your bulletins, especially everything that Anna had written. Isn't it galactic that her school had the same name as your district! My district is called Uppsala. I wonder if there was a school in Uppsala two hundred years ago. Wouldn't it be solar if there had been students there who had buried a time capsule, too?

I was looking at some of the two-dimensional images — you know, those things called photographs. Did you notice that some of the people were wearing glass and wire eye-coverings? Plutonian! I checked these out in the data bank and discovered that people with eye defects had to wear things called glasses. Perhaps they didn't know about laser surgery back then.

Anyway, it got me thinking. I'd like to contribute to your time capsule by providing a project on medical science. It's so much more advanced now. But I suppose one hundred years from now, maybe it will seem old-fashioned. Who knows?

Your new friend : Sweda : End of message

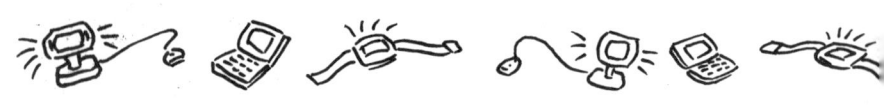

Advances in Medical Science

Bionic Limb Research

Cancer Research

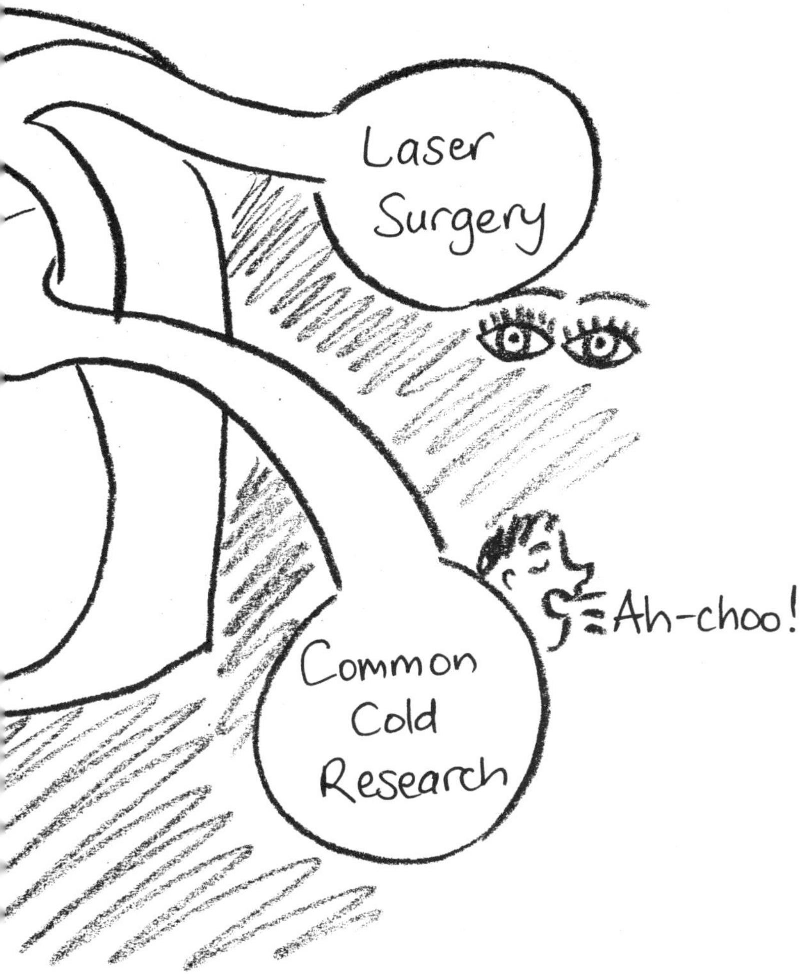
Laser Surgery
Ah-choo!
Common Cold Research

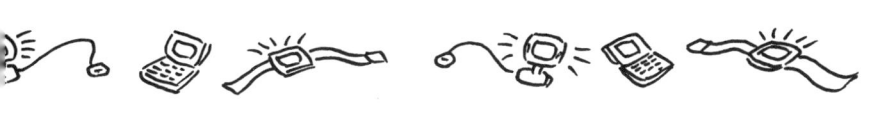

Seleka, Taka, and Ronka

> *Earth time : 1700 hours*
> *Saturday : May 13, 2198*
>
> **Instructions to Personal Data Assistant**
>
> *Record thought waves as transmitted, translate to text in all Earth languages, and store on long-lasting FIP discs for retrieval in the year 2298.*

Dear Future,

Well, today I thought I'd tell you a bit more about my life in the unit and what I do during the day. I share my cubicle with three ten-year-olds: Seleka, Taka, and Ronka.

Each morning, I wake up to the sound of music on the multiscreen in our cubicle. It is only a very small one – nothing like the huge one in the learning center. I put on my exersuit and travel by moving sidewalk to the exeroom on level 27. Then I start my fitness program – I jog on a treadmill, lift weights, and stretch my limbs.

Phew!

On the way out of the exeroom, we are given a package containing meal one. It is made up of capsules that have been nutritionally enriched, and fibrous substances that taste quite pleasant. Meals two and three come at regular intervals throughout the day – more capsules. We also receive protein- and calcium-enriched liquids.

I had never even thought about my meals until I read about the types of food that Anna's class enjoyed. Then I really started to think about it.

So I went to the ROM Room and selected a ROM about how food was produced. I found out that, up until halfway through the twentieth century, people grew their own food on places called farms. And some farms stocked animals, which were also used for food. Can you imagine getting food from an animal? I can't.

All our food is synthetically produced in a lab. According to the ROM, the radiation that had leaked from nuclear power plants in the 2040s meant that it wasn't safe for food to be grown in the soil. Farm animals were also affected, because they had eaten grain from the poisoned soil. Animals don't provide humans with food anymore.

I also found images of people eating spaghetti, which was one of the recipes from Anna's time capsule. Oh, how I would like to try it!

But back to my day. After exercise, we go to the learning center. We spend the morning with Viki, using SIMs to find out about the outside world, and how society works. Then, after meal two, we go to the technology unit and learn how to program the different robots who will work for us during our lives.

I have to tell you all about XC50, my personal-training robot. I spend so much time with it, I guess you could almost call it my friend!

XC50 was assigned to me when I turned five, and entered the junior training unit. Everybody has one. But I think XC50 is special. Its job is to introduce me to all the robots, then train me to operate them.

Constructors build things.

Domservers wash and clean.

Retrievers look after materials in the central data bank and Rom Rooms.

Demomats knock things down and remove rubble.

Why do I think XC50 is special? Well, it seems to have more "personality" than other XC models. I guess it means being like a "person."

← my
XC50
what

And you wouldn't expect robots to actually be like people, would you? I mean, they're just a collection of computer chips and wires and circuits. But XC50's eyes seem to twinkle at me. Well, they're not really eyes, they're TV screens that scan images and send messages back to the electronic brain.

But this morning, something terrible happened! One of XC50's circuits malfunctioned. It has to go to the repair unit to get fixed. I'm really going to miss it. The learning center has assigned me one of the newer TY models to fill in while it's gone, but life just won't be the same.

For a start, TY86 doesn't know any songs. XC50 is always singing me songs. One of XC50's previous students programed music from the last two centuries into its data banks, and every now and then it reproduces some of them for me.

My Favorite Songs

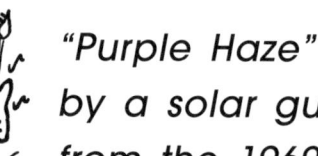

"Purple Haze"
by a solar guitarist
from the 1960s
named Jimi Hendrix.

"Wannabe"
by an all-female group
from the 1990s
called Spice Girls.

"Rings around Saturn"
by a group of colonists
from the 2140s
called Space Junk.

Do you like music, dear person of the future? Have you heard of any of my favorite songs? They're all much better than the boring electronic bips that come out of my multiscreen every morning. Music isn't nearly as good as it used to be. I wonder what sort of music you play in your time.

Anika : End of message

> *Earth time : 0900 hours*
> *Monday : May 15, 2198*
> *To Anika : Cubicle 47 :*
> *   Sector 813 : Unit #2779369K*
> *From Roq : Cubicle 28 :*
> *   Sector 452 : Unit #29966884Q*
>
> **Instructions to Personal Data Assistant**
>
> *Translate from French to English and alert user to existence of incoming message.*

Hi, Anika! My name is Roq. I think it's just so extraterrestrial that you're making a time capsule. And I loved reading all about Anna's class.

What funny games they played back then — jump rope, marbles, and tag? Really outer-Plutonian! But I guess game technology just wasn't as advanced as it is now. Well, that's not really their fault.

I've sent you a project about our games to go into your time capsule. I've also included a few SIMs so that the people of the future can play them for themselves. I put in hover hockey (my favorite) and skatorama. I think they'll really enjoy this game, even if it is only in virtual reality. The best places I've skated on so far are the Eiffel Tower (here in the Paris District), the Great Pyramids of the Egypt District, and the Empire State Building in the New York District. How about you?

Keep up the good work, Anika. Can you send me details of how I can contact the other kids? I'd like to chat with them.

See you! : Roq : End of message

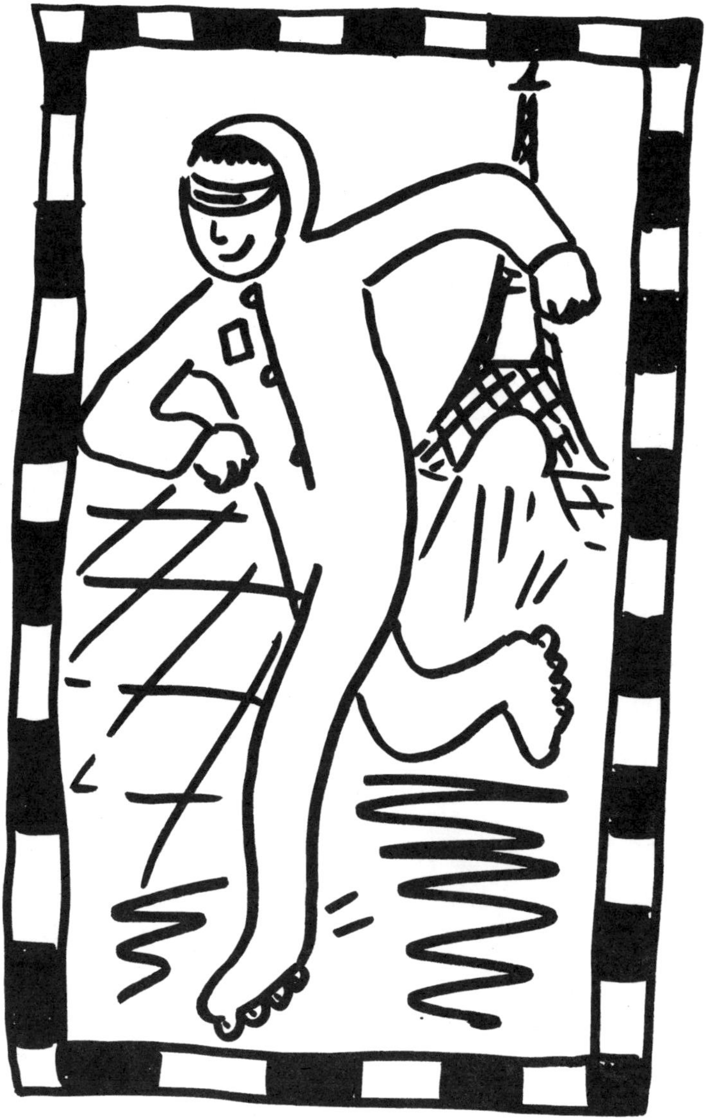

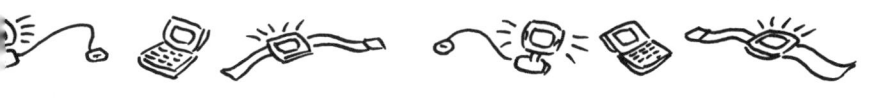

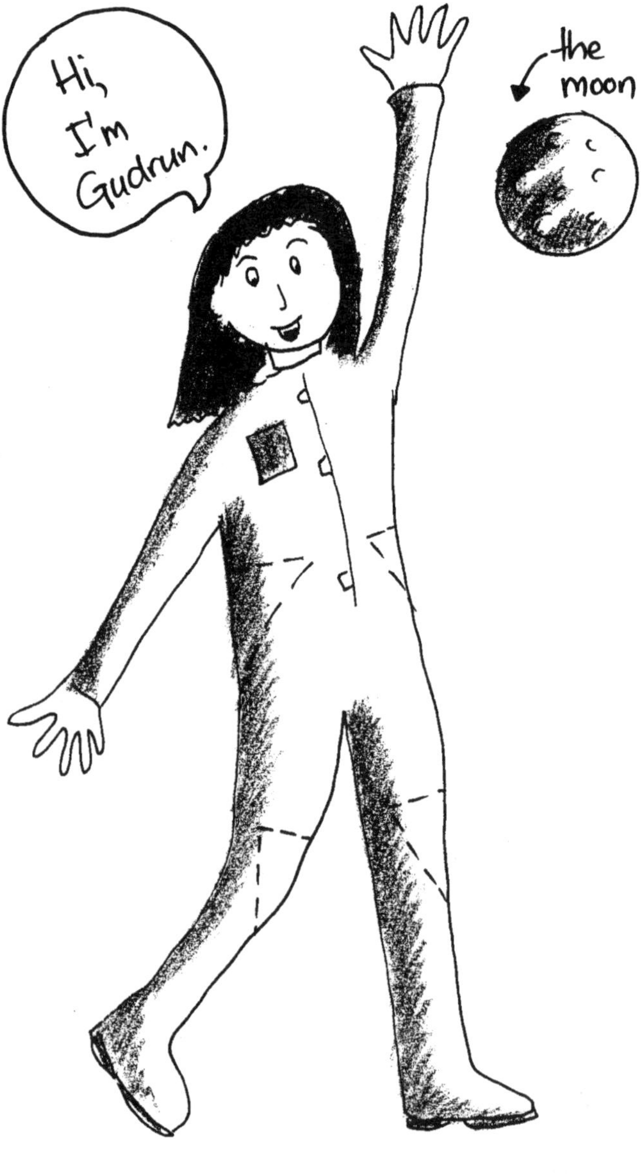
Hi, I'm Gudrun.
the moon

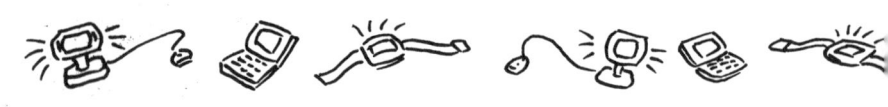

> *Earth time : 0930 hours*
> *Monday : May 15, 2198*
> *To Anika : Cubicle 47 :*
> *   Sector 813 : Unit #2779369K*
> *From Gudrun : Basecamp :*
> *   Lunar Colony 3*
>
> ### *Instructions to Personal Data Assistant*
> *Translate from Lunaspeak to English and alert user to existence of incoming message.*

Hi, Anika. This is Gudrun. I'm a fifth-generation colonist from the moon, so I can only speak Lunaspeak. However, I've asked my PDA to translate my message into English for you.

We don't have as many resources here on the moon as you do, but we have a good data bank. I'm always getting into trouble for looking up what Earth used to be like, when I'm supposed to be studying rock samples. My colony is near the big mining fields of the Sea of Tranquility.

You know what you said about wanting to find out about your ancestors? Well, I've discovered lots of new things about my family on this great program called FamilyTrace on the SolarNet. You see, we still follow many of the old ways. We don't live in units, like you do. My family and the other people at basecamp live in domes that have controlled atmospheres and gravity factors. When we go outside, we have to wear our space suits all the time.

← Here is my dome.

My mom gave me a few names to start the program. And I found out that one of the original colonists was my great-great-great-grandfather. His name was Alfred Pickles, and he was a mining engineer. That's why he came to the moon one hundred years ago — to work in the mines. His daughter, Zelda, took over for him, and I guess when I'm old enough I'll carry on the family tradition, too. There aren't very many other occupations here, not yet, anyway!

Alfred Pickles

So maybe you could call up the search program and trace your own family.

Anyway, I've included a project for the time capsule. You know how you said you couldn't keep personal possessions because there wasn't enough space? Well, that's not a problem for me here at Lunar Colony 3.

I've started a collection of space debris and moon trivia! I found some of the articles while zooming around the basecamp in my hovercraft, and others at souvenir stalls at Landing 1.

Bye for now : Gudrun : End of message

My Collection of Space Debris and Moon Trivia

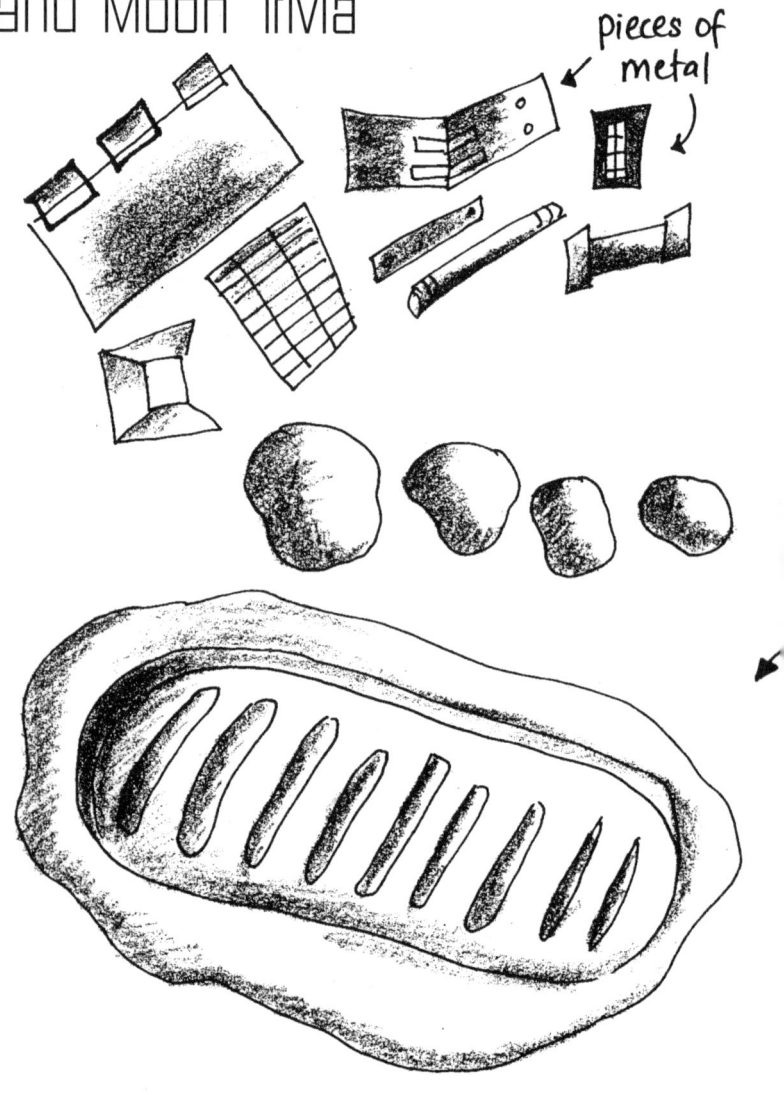

pieces of metal

meteorites

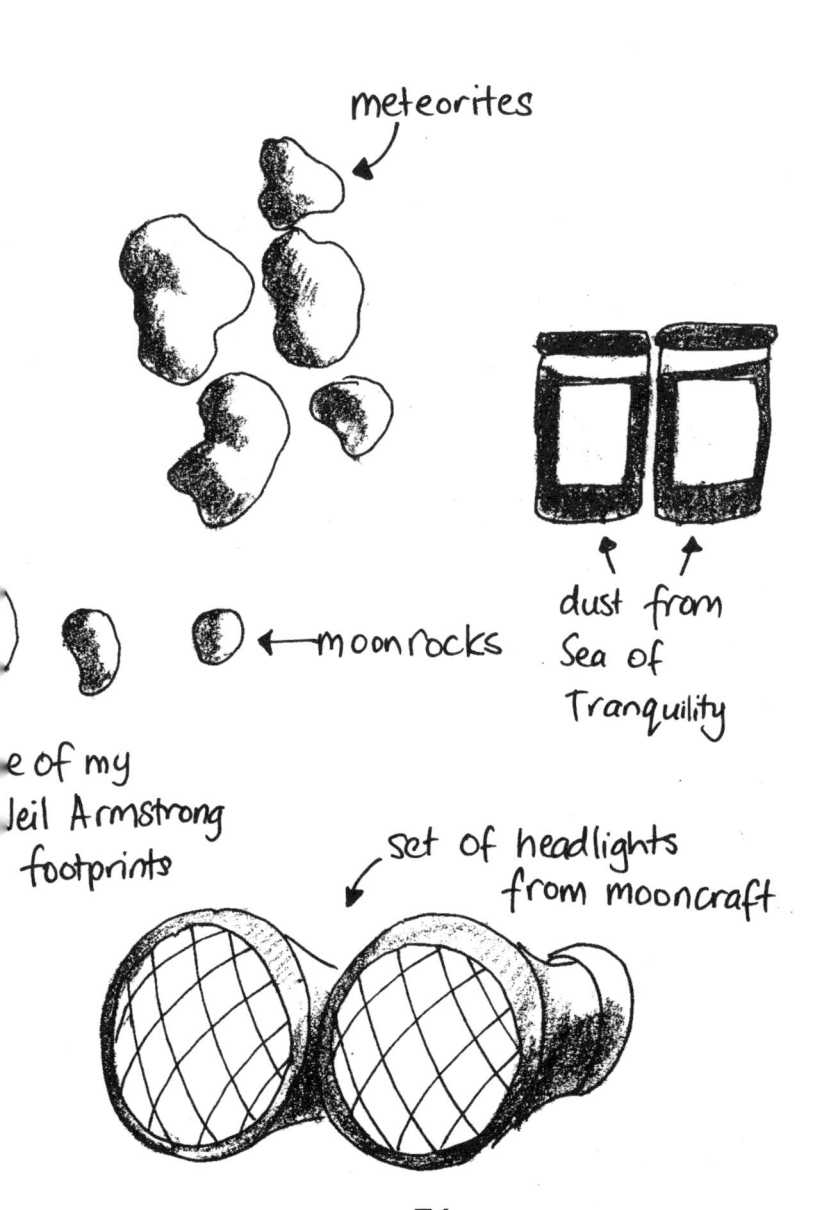

dust from
Sea of
Tranquility

← moonrocks

e of my
Jeil Armstrong
footprints

set of headlights
from mooncraft

71

> *Earth time : 1706 hours*
> *Monday : May 15, 2198*
>
> ***Instructions to Personal Data Assistant***
>
> *Record thought waves as transmitted, translate to text in all Earth languages, and store on long-lasting FIP discs for retrieval in the year 2298.*

Dear Future,

Oh, I'm so worried. This morning when I checked the news bulletin on the multiscreen in my cubicle, it said that repairs to XC50 hadn't been finished.

Even worse, my XC50 might get recycled. I can't bear it! A similar thing happened to Ronka's XC robot. One of its circuits malfunctioned, so it was sent to the repair unit to be fixed. Only, it never came back. The technicians decided it would take too much time and too many resources to repair the robot. Instead, Ronka was issued a new TY model, and XC33 was used for spare parts.

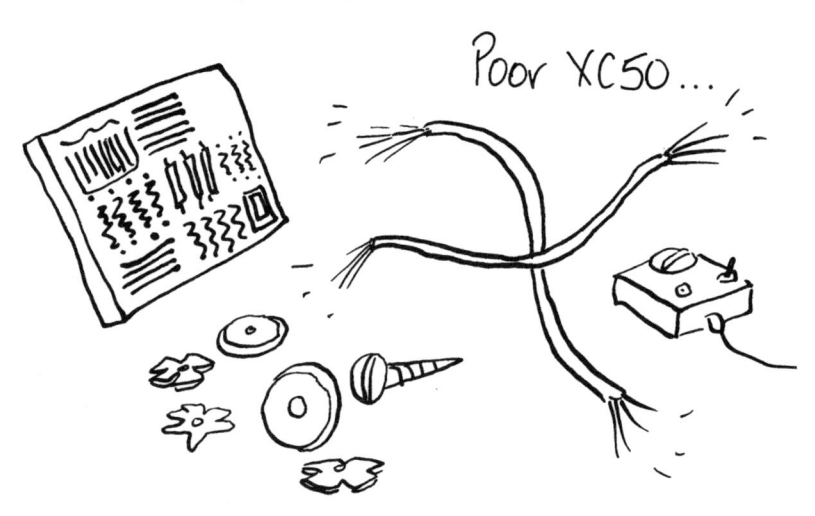

Poor XC50...

Ronka can't understand why I'm so upset. She says robots don't have feelings, just information that's programed by their controllers. She says her TY15 can do tons of things her XC33 couldn't.

But I don't care about having a TY robot that walks on two legs rather than shuffling around on six. And I hate to think of poor old XC50 waiting on the repair line. And I don't agree with what Ronka says about robots not having feelings. XC50 does, I'm sure of it. Perhaps some sort of glitch occurred when the technicians were assembling it. Or maybe it just learned its behavior from being around me. Viki says I have more "feelings" than anyone else in my unit. I wonder why I'm so different.

But I'm glad I have feelings. I'm glad I can be happy when I see my parents, or when Viki lets us travel back in time in a SIM. But, you know, the opposite of happiness is sadness. And you can't have one without the other. So, I feel sad about some things, too. Like the fact that I don't live with my parents, like Anna did.

I've made a reservation for tomorrow to use the SolarNet. It's really hard to get on sometimes; everyone wants to use it at the same time. It's a lot of fun being hooked up to computers all over the solar system. The last time I used it, I chatted with some people on Jupiter Colony.

But tomorrow, I'm going to use the search program for FamilyTrace, the program that Gudrun told me about. What if I find out I was related to someone really important?

Or maybe I'm related to one of the great writers from the past. There must be at least a few writers' genes in me, don't you think?

I'll write again tomorrow. It's time for meal three. Capsules again. If only I could try some chocolate cake, or spaghetti, or fried rice. People back then just don't know how good they had it!

Anika : End of message

Asia — Vietnam

> *Earth time : 0945 hours*
> *Tuesday : May 16, 2198*
> *To Anika : Cubicle 47 :*
> *   Sector 813 : Unit #2779369K*
> *From Nyoc : Cubicle 76 :*
> *   Sector 421 : Unit #2795444C*
>
> **Instructions to Personal Data Assistant**
>
> *Translate from Vietnamese to English and alert user to existence of incoming message.*

Hi, Anika! Nyoc here, from Unit #2795444C. I've been trying to get through to you for a few days, but your response bank is jammed. You must be getting lots of messages!

I was sent some messages from some of the other kids from units around the globe. I even got some from a few of the outer colonies. Thanks! I think we should all arrange to have a Netchat some night. What do you think? Wouldn't that be galactic? We could all book space on the SolarNet and log on at the same time. I've been wondering if there were other kids *Out There* who thought like I do. And, now that I know that there are, I don't want to lose touch with any of you. So let's do it.

I also wanted to make a contribution to the time capsule. I've attached a clothing project. I see what you mean about the clothes from Anna's time being scratchy! Using fiber from animals or plants seems so odd.

What's even weirder is that they had to iron them! Jupiter's moons! I'll contact you soon about the SolarNet idea. Keep cool (as Anna would say).

Your new friend : Nyoc : End of message

Nyoc's Clothing Project

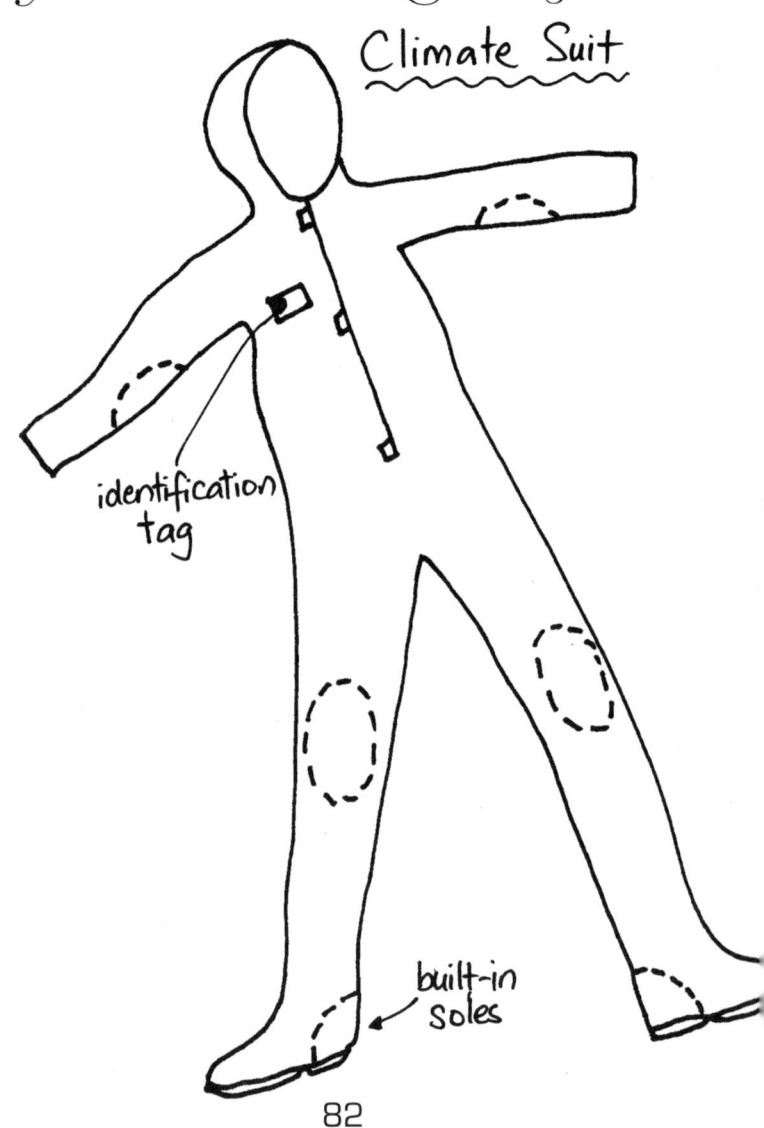

Climate Suit

identification tag

built-in soles

82

Exersuit

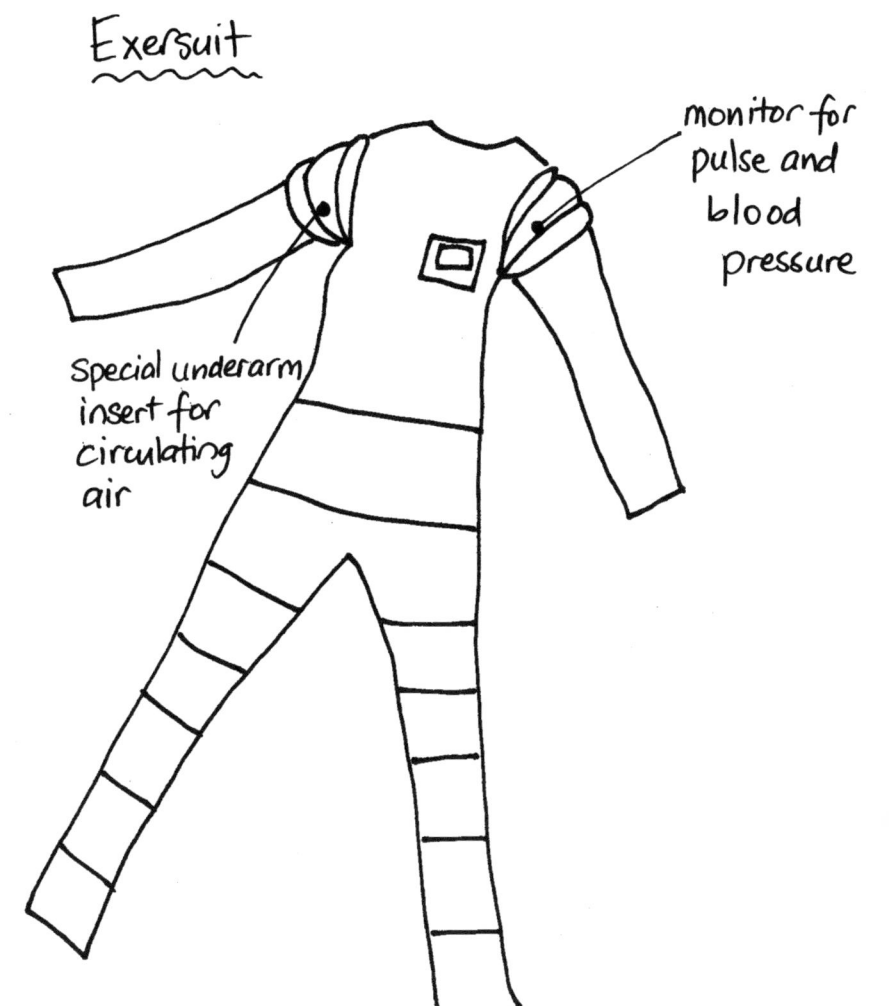

monitor for pulse and blood pressure

special underarm insert for circulating air

Earth time : 1706 hours
Tuesday : May 16, 2198

Instructions to Personal Data Assistant

Record thought waves as transmitted, translate to text in all Earth languages, and store on long-lasting FIP discs for retrieval in the year 2298.

Dear Future,

Oh, I've got so much news for you today! You'll never believe what has happened. I'm finding it hard to believe, myself. I'm not even sure where to start.

First of all, XC50 has been reprieved! They're not going to recycle it or consign it to craterfill. I heard the news on my multiscreen news bulletin this morning. Apparently, they found that there was only a minor problem with the circuits. All it took was a few quick adjustments of the rotordrive and everything was cool again. See, even *I'm* starting to talk like Anna now. I think it must be catching!

So XC50 was back when I reported for our afternoon session. It was waiting in the line for me to activate it. I thought its eyes had an extra twinkle in them when I came into the room. Do you think that's possible?

And then there's the other news. I can't wait to tell you the other news. It's just, well, it's more than galactic, it's *universal!*

You see, this afternoon I looked up the FamilyTrace program. Now, because I don't have a surname, only a number like everyone else in *New World*, the program had to match my number to all sorts of coded information. But finally it found my last ancestor to use a surname. The name appeared on the screen.

Reynard!

That was my family's surname before people lost their last names and were given unit numbers instead.

Anika Reynard, Unit #2779369K

I kept looking at the name on the screen. It seemed familiar, but I couldn't figure out why. And then it hit me right between the eyes, with the force of a well-placed hover hockey shot. Anna's surname was Reynard. *Anna Loredana Eugenia Hope Reynard.* We had the same surname!

I was so excited, I had to let XC50 take over and key in the next program command. I felt this wetness on my face, just below my eyes. What was it and how did it get there? I hadn't brought any liquids into the SolarNet room with me.

After a few more minutes of computations, the screen revealed a string of names, showing my ancestors way back to when records first began in *Old World*. There were all sorts of interesting names. But, there was only one that really interested me, and that was Anna's name. Anna is one of my ancestors. Can you believe it? Anna and I are related.

And you know, it makes sense, doesn't it? Remember how I thought I must be related to someone who liked writing? Anna liked writing. Well, she wrote a journal, just like I have. That's what she chose to put in the time capsule. A journal. Just like I'm doing.

And you know what? I'm going to put her real journal in the time capsule, not just a hologram of it. That way you can get to see what a *real* book was like. Hold it in your hands, maybe, and feel its soft cover and smooth pages. Just like I was able to do.

Will you promise me something, dear person of the future? Will you start another time capsule, too? Will you keep a journal so that in another hundred years people will have a record of what your life was like?

And one more thing. Will you pass Anna's book on, as I did?

Good-bye and good luck to you in the future.

Your friend : Anika : End of message

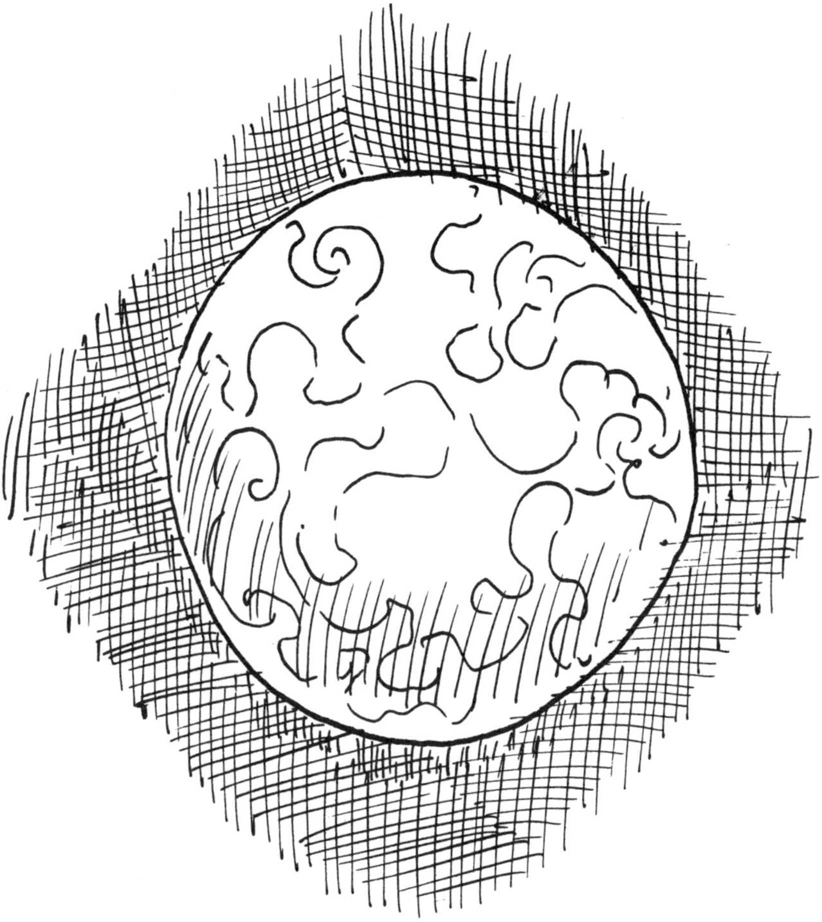

From the Author

When I was invited to write a sequel to *Dear Future,* I thought a lot about how I was going to do it. How can we possibly know what the future will be like? So I decided to do some research. I talked to historians, science-fiction writers, and students.

Everyone had different ideas, and all of them were interesting. Maybe someone from the future will come across this book one day and find a way of letting me know what they think of it!

Meredith Costain

From the Illustrator

It was lots of fun illustrating *The Journal: Dear Future II*. For each illustration, I pretended I was the character doing the drawing. I had to imagine what it felt like to be Anika, and then draw from her point of view.

The Journal: Dear Future II presented the extra challenge of drawing a world that hasn't happened yet! Well, what would a house on the moon look like? If I lived in Anika's time, I'd live on the moon.

Teresa Culkin-Lawrence

ANOTHER TIME, ANOTHER PLACE
Cloudcatcher
Flags
The Dinosaur Connection
Myth or Mystery?
Where Did the Maya Go?
The Journal: Dear Future II

CONFIDENCE AND COURAGE
Imagine This, James Robert
Follow That Spy!
Who Will Look Out for Danny?
Fuzz and the Glass Eye
Bald Eagles
Cottle Street

SOMETHING STRANGE
My Father the Mad Professor
A Theft in Time: Timedetectors II
CD and the Giant Cat
Chocolate!
White Elephants and Yellow Jackets
Dream Boat

WHEN THINGS GO WRONG
The Long Walk Home
The Trouble with Patrick
The Kids from Quiller's Bend
Laughter Is the Best Medicine
Wild Horses
The Sunday Horse

Written by **Meredith Costain**
Illustrated by **Teresa Culkin-Lawrence**
Edited by **Ann-Marie Heffernan**
Designed by **Nicola Evans**

Photography by **Photopia Images**: (p. 39; p. 61; p. 81);
Sarah Irvine: (p. 32)

© 1997 Shortland Publications Limited
All rights reserved.

02 01 00 99 98 97
10 9 8 7 6 5 4 3 2 1

Distributed in the United States by
   Rigby
   a division of Reed Elsevier Inc.
   P.O. Box 797
   Crystal Lake, IL 60039-0797

Printed by Colorcraft, Hong Kong
ISBN: 0-7901-1684-7